God's Extended Hand

40-day Devotional Journal to Help You Overcome the Storm

KEISHA BROWN

God's Extended Hand: 40-day devotional journal to help you overcome the storm.

Copyright © 2022 by Keisha Brown

All rights reserved. No part of this publvication may be reproduced, distributed, or transmitted in any form or by any means, including photocopying, recording, or other electronic or mechanical methods, or by any information storage and retrieval system without the prior written permission of the author, except in the case of very brief quotations embodied in the critical reviews and certain other noncommercial uses permitted by copyright law.

Unless otherwise indicated, Scripture quotations are taken from the Holy Bible New International Version. Copyright ©1973,1978,1984 by International Bible Society. Used by permission of Zondervan Publishing House.

Scripture quotations marked ESV are taken from the Holy Bible, English Standard Version. Copyright © 2001 by Crossway, a publishing ministry of Good News Publishers. Used by permission. All rights reserved.

Cover photo: Ivan Bandura/Unsplash

PREFACE

God's Extended Hand is designed to provide a lifeline to help you out of your raging storm. If you are feeling alone and afraid, then open your heart to accept the help only God can provide. I, too, went through a time when I felt like the world around me was filled with nothing but misery and pain. I can still remember the day so vividly of me sitting in my car overcome with so much emotion that all I could do was weep hysterically. It was in that despair that my miracle happened. As I cried out in desperation for God to save me, the most amazing thing happened. He did. He reached out His hand to me, picked me up and led me out of the darkness. From that moment, all I could do was put one foot in front of the other, take one day at a time and let God lead me toward freedom.

This journey will take you through the cleansing process, developing a new identity, persevering through the struggles and so much more. All you have to do is open your heart to God's promise for your life.

INTRODUCTION

Don't spend another day with the hurt, anger, or loneliness you are feeling. Life is meant to be enjoyed, not feel like a burden. It's time to calm the storm. God wants to cleanse you and take away your pain and suffering to start fresh. He has a promise for your life that He wants to share with you, but you must open your heart to receive it.

This devotional journal is designed to help you create a devotion, bible study and prayer routine that works for you. Use the journal to express yourself, reflect, and grow. Writing in your journal is a great way to nurture your creativity, make sense of your thoughts, and develop a deeper understanding of yourself and your life as you make time to devote to the Lord. Enjoy this time to connect with God in a meaningful way.

Here is how to get the most out of your devotional journal:

1. Start by setting a goal for your devotion journey. For example, "What do I want to learn or achieve by the end of the 40 days?" or "I want to spend 20 minutes in devotion and bible study time each day."

2. Plan your day the night before beginning with your devotion and bible study time and include your goals for the day.

3. Set aside time to read the devotion for the day and pray. Use the journal pages to catalog your thoughts and revelations.

4. Reflect on the bible passage for the day; include how you can apply it to your life and your feelings both positive and negative as honestly and openly as possible.

5. Write each day. Be creative! You can write in paragraphs, draw pictures, or make lists.

6. Choose a time and place that's comfortable and free from distractions.

7. Listen to hear God's voice in your study time; write down His messages to you.

8. At the end of the 40 days, look back at your entries and reflect on what God has done in your life!

The road to freedom is not an easy one. It takes courage, perseverance, and faith. There will be stumbles along the way, but one thing is for sure, it is worth what God will do for you.

Embrace an attitude of: "Lord, I want to hear from you. I want to change my life" and God will extend His hand to you.

Grab Hold of God's Hand

"The Lord saw how great man's wickedness on the earth had become, and that every inclination of the thoughts of his heart was only evil all the time."
-Genesis 6:5

Day 1

Know God

"Seek first His kingdom and His righteousness, and all these things will be given to you as well." -Matthew 6:33

To begin this process, first things first, you must be saved.

Have you accepted Jesus as your savior? If you have, great! If you are unsure, now is a perfect time to commit or recommit your life to Christ.

Experiencing the change, you are looking for, will require God's help. Take the time to accept Jesus into your life. And if you already have, decide to build on your relationship. Pray this prayer to commit or recommit your life to the Lord.

Heavenly Father

I come to you in prayer asking for the forgiveness of my sins. I confess with my mouth that Jesus is Lord and I believe in my heart that You raised Him from the dead. I thank you Lord that you sent your only begotten Son, Jesus, to die on the cross for me so that I would have eternal life. Come into my heart today, Heavenly Father, that I may begin to live with purpose and to bring glory to Your kingdom. With this confession, I am now cleansed by the blood of Jesus, and I will praise you all the days of my life.

In Jesus' Name, Amen.

"That if you confess with your mouth, "Jesus is Lord," and believe in heart that God raised Him from the dead, you will be saved. For it is with your heart that you believe and are justified, and it is with your mouth that you confess and are saved." -Romans 10:9-10

What is your relationship with God? Do you have one? If you do, do you put Him first? What things are you putting before Him?

Day 2

Create a Clean Slate

"If we confess our sins, His is faithful and just and will forgive us our sins and purify us from all unrighteousness." -I John 1:9

Creating a clean slate means dealing with past offenses. You must get rid of the sin in your life. It may be one thing in particular or a couple of things. Whatever it is, it needs to go. Confess your sins before God, and let that be the end of it. The devil will try to hold your past sins over your head. Don't let him. Tell him that you have been forgiven and they no longer exist in your life and are no longer remembered by God. (Psalm 103:12) I am not saying it is going to be easy. It may be a habit you're trying to quit, and you continue to slip up. Keep asking for God's help and He will see you through. The biggest challenge will be to forgive yourself especially if you keep making the same mistake or have harmed someone because of your sin. Once you allow yourself to accept God's forgiveness and forgive yourself your faith gets stronger and the less the devil can attack you in this area. Do not let sin have control in your life. (Psalm 119:133)

Accept that your forgiveness and press forward to what is ahead. (Philippians 3:13b)

"For I will forgive their wickedness and will remember their sins no more."
-Hebrews 8:12

Have you asked for God's forgiveness? Have you forgiven yourself? Use your journal to express your feelings and work through your emotions as you let go of your past.

Day 3

Spend Time Reading The Bible

"May the words of my mouth and the meditation of my heart be pleasing in your sight. O Lord, my Rock, my Redeemer" -Psalm 19:14

Yesterday, you opened your heart to want to receive direction. But now you may be wondering, where does the direction come from? It will come from God's word. All you have to do is open it up. You do not have to start at the beginning. Find YOUR starting point. As you begin to read, God will speak to your heart and reveal what the words mean for your life. You are no longer just reading words on a page but meditating on their meaning. Direction will soon follow. Don't get discouraged if it doesn't happen right away. Keep reading and write down in your journal meaningful scriptures for your reference. The important thing is taking time to be still and listen to what God is saying in your heart. Do you find that when you pray, you do all the talking? A true relationship is a two-way street allowing the other person to speak too.

Try and start your day with prayer and bible meditation. If that means waking up a little earlier- do it!

Do you think you need to speak less and listen more? Try it.

"Open my eyes that I may see wonderful things in your law."
-Psalm 119:18

Take time to write down what you want to get out of this process. Set goals for yourself.

Day 4

Purify Your Heart

"Create in me a pure heart, O God, and renew a steadfast spirit within me." -Psalm 51:10

What does it mean to have a pure heart? It means your motives are sincere. When your heart is pure you are doing things to benefit others not yourself. Are you the type of person that only does something for someone to get something in return? Examine your heart, be real with yourself about why you do things. Then ask God to create in you a pure heart. When you start putting the needs of others in front of your own, your outlook changes. You stop needing the approval of others because the only approval you need is from God.

Strive to make your life less about what you want and more about what God wants for you. God's plan for your life is so much better than anything you could want for yourself. He created you, so He knows what is best for you. Trust the Lord to provide what is best for you.

"Now to Him who is able to do immeasurably more than all we ask or imagine, according to His power that is at work within us."
-Ephesians 3:20

Have you been asking God to bless your plans, or is it time you asked God for His plan?

Day 5

Open Your Heart To His Direction

"In his heart a man plans his course, but the Lord determines his steps."
-Proverbs 16:9

Something has brought you to this point of wanting a significant change in your life, make the decision to take time to work through it. Be committed to this journey. Have an expectation for God to do amazing things in this process. Allow God to lead you and be open to His direction. It is going to be a challenge, but the best accomplishments in life come through patience and effort. Think back to a time when you wanted something and did everything it took to get it. The blood, sweat and tears you put in to see it through. Now remember how you felt when you achieved it. If you put in the work over the next forty days, the result will be even better than that!

Trust in the Lord's plan, He only wants what is best for you.

Ask God to give you direction and the courage to do it.

"For I know the plans I have for you, declares the Lord, plans to prosper you and not to harm you, plans to give you hope and a future."
-Jeremiah 29:11

What changes will you make in your life to make time for this process? What are you believing God to do for you?

Day 6

Commit Your Day To The Lord

"Commit to the Lord whatever you do, and your plans will succeed."
-Proverbs 16:3

You have now begun to work on designing a new routine. I'm sure it is taking some getting used to. Working out a few kinks, perhaps you were not even able to do three days in a row. That is ok. Just keep trying. There are going to be things that get in the way of allowing you to do what you need to do. Take a moment to give your day over to God. Let Him help you in every area, big or small. He cares about what you care about. I remember a day I wanted a peach so bad. I hadn't had one in a really long time, and I just had a craving for one. There was no way for me to go get one because I was working all day. So, I just put it out of my mind. After lunch, one of my co-workers came over to me and said they had a left-over peach from their lunch and offered it to me. The way I reacted you would have thought she brought me a thousand dollars. But in that moment, I realized how much God really cares about what I care about. I didn't even ask Him for it. He just wanted to give me what I wanted.

Don't allow the troubles you may experience at work or other daily activities weigh you down. You may not be satisfied on your job or perhaps you are unemployed. Whatever situation you are in, stay productive, give 100% to your tasks. Do it as if Jesus were sitting right next to you. (Colossians 3:23) If you are asking God to change your situation, be patient. Allow God to make a way in His time.

"Cast all your anxiety on Him because He cares for you."
-I Peter 5:7

What is weighing you down that you want God to take away?

Day 7

Change Your Mind

"Do not conform any longer to the pattern of this world but be transformed by the renewing of your mind. Then you will be able to test and approve God's will is-His good, pleasing and perfect will." -Romans 12:2

There are two parts to this scripture. First, you have to "renew your mind", in other words, refresh the way you think, in order to change the way you behave. Your brain is very powerful, to change the way you operate in your daily life, your brain must change what it is drawn to do. You may tend to say, "I won't have dessert after dinner", instead of saying "I will go for a walk after dinner." When you think in terms of what you won't do, you are focusing on the activity that you are trying to stop. Rather than your focus being on what you should do. You have to control what you allow to take up space in your mind. That is why it so important to get into your daily habit of meditation on His word. This will renew your mind every morning and experience God's peace and love. (Lamentations 3:22-23) As you get closer to Him, He gets closer to you.

"Come near to God and He will come near to you."
-James 4:8a

Where do you need to change your focus of thinking? Be more positive. Change the direction of your thinking from "I won't(s)" to "I will(s)".

Find Favor with God

"But Noah found favor in the eyes of the Lord."
-Genesis 6:8

Day 8

Righteousness

"Noah was a righteous man, blameless among the people of his time, and he walked with God." -Genesis 6:9

Why did God save Noah? Plainly, Noah did what was right. He lived his life pleasing to God. His habits and daily living were in obedience to God's commands. He was a man of virtue and good character. How do you know what is right? You learn it from the bible. "All Scripture is God-breathed and is useful for teaching, rebuking, correcting and training in righteousness." II Timothy 3:16

Righteousness is obedience to God's word. Let it guide you in your daily walk. Appreciate the bible for being more than verses to get you through the day when you in trouble or in need, but as a guide for everyday living. That is how to develop a relationship with God. We are a tool, a vessel to be used for His glory. Accept that without Jesus we have nothing. Open your heart to His words and it will put you on the path to righteousness in Christ.

Do you only look for scriptures that are encouraging and uplifting? Look for ones that cause correction. Allow God to teach you. Write down the lessons you receive.

"And if we are careful to obey all this law before the Lord our God, as He commanded us, that will be our righteousness"
-Deuteronomy 6:25

Allow God to teach you. Write down what He is saying to you.

Day 9

Act In Obedience

"If you love Me, you will obey what I command." -John 14:15

Obedience is a tough word to hear. Part of you is ingrained to want to rebel. You don't want to be told what to do. But God wants you to put aside that thinking for Him. Everything God tells you do is for your protection and wellbeing. God has no other motive than His pure love for you. And in return, God asks you to obey to show your love for Him.

Think about the areas God revealed to you to cleanse. Do not put off what He has commanded you to do. Yes, it will be difficult. Obedience will test your strength and will power. Habits form over years. They become second nature; you may not even realize you are doing them. God wants you to lean on Him to break these habits. He will be with you, and you can overcome. "In all things we are more than conquerors through Him who loved us." -Romans 8:37

Continue to make time to read God's word and let it fill your heart. Let Him strengthen you to stay the course. "I can do all things through Christ which gives me strength." -Philippians 4:13 (KJV)

"My grace is sufficient for you, for My power is made perfect in weakness. Therefore, I will boast all the more gladly about my weaknesses, so that Christ's power may rest on me. That is why, for Christ's sake, I delight in weaknesses, in insults, in hardships, in persecutions, in difficulties. For when I am weak, then I am strong." -II Corinthians 12:9-10

Write down the areas you are struggling to be obedient and give them over to God.

Day 10

Blamelessness

"Lord, who may dwell in your sanctuary? Who may live on your holy hill? He whose walk is blameless and who does what is righteous, who speaks the truth from his heart." -Psalm 15:1-2

To be blameless is not to be without sin. It is to overcome sin through confession and repentance. Asking God to forgive our sins is what cleanses you and removes your guilt. You can then move forward to do better. Keep your heart pure and your motives in line with the word of God.

Noah was "blameless among the people of his time". (Genesis 6:9) I'm sure that was not easy. There was sin and evil all around him, but he remained diligent in his obedience to God's commands. He put God first in his life, and he was rewarded for his efforts. You are facing the same challenges today. There is evil and sin all around you. Are you doing what is right? When you misstep, are you asking for forgiveness? Be the one who stands out and finds favor with the Lord.

"Do you not know that in a race all the runners run, but only one gets the prize? Run in such a way as to get the prize."
-I Corinthians 9:24

What areas do you feel the pressures around you? What steps can you take to maintain discipline in your walk?x

Day 11

Be Joyful Always

"Do everything without complaining or arguing, so that you my become blameless and pure, children of God without fault in a crooked and depraved generation, in which you shine like stars in the universe"
-Philippians 2:14-15

Joyful does not mean happy. Happy is circumstantial. When a situation changes or doesn't go our way you can easily become unhappy. Joy is state of being. No matter the circumstance you heart is filled with contentment and peace knowing everything will be alright.

Noah was among an evil and corrupt generation, so are you. And just as Noah, you are meant to shine like stars in the universe. Let the joy of Lord and peace in your heart shine through. Changing your habits and routines gets difficult but stay focused on your attitude. Hold tight to your goal and know that it will be worth it. Your tendency may be to complain or gripe because you hit a roadblock. But don't, they are inevitable.

Following these three steps (1. Be joyful always 2. Pray continually 3. Give thanks in all circumstances) will get you through any situation that is causing you to become discouraged.

"Be joyful always; pray continually; give thanks in all circumstances, for this is God's will for you in Christ Jesus."
-I Thessalonians 5:16-18

Write down things you are most thankful for that you can refer to in times of struggle? As you study God's word, write down scriptures to use as you pray.

Day 12

Walk With God- Allow God To Set Your Path

"The Lord Himself goes before you and will be with you, He will never leave you nor forsake you. Do not be afraid; do not be discouraged."
-Deuteronomy 31:8

What does it mean to walk with God? Think about when you take a walk with a friend, what happens? You share stories, laugh, and enjoy each other's company. When you walk with God, it means you have developed a relationship with Him and developing a relationship requires trust. You feel free to share your victories and your concerns. Keep in mind, relationships are two-way streets. You can't be the one talking all the time. You should also listen to what God has to say to you. So, how do you build that relationship? 1) Allow God to set the path for your walk 2) Obey His Word and 3) When you make a mistake, ask for forgiveness, and get right back on the path.

God is always with you. He has laid out a path for you that although it will not be free of trials, it will be exactly what you need to grow and mature. Your walk with God is perfectly designed for the goal He has in mind for you. Do not let circumstances around you dictate your moves. Stay the course and continue to let your instruction come from God.

"I will instruct you and teach you in the way you should go. I will counsel you and watch over you."
-Psalm 32:8

Examine your current walk with God. Who is directing the path? Ask God for direction today.

Day 13

Walk with God- Obey His Word

"This is love for God: to obey His commands and His commands are not burdensome." -I John 5:3

The second part of walking with God is to do what He tells you. This is how you show your love and trust that God knows what is best for you. You must obey all parts of the bible not just the parts you agree with or the things that come easy. It means listening when the Holy Spirit whispers in your ear to do something or not do something. The more you tune in to the spirit within you, the more you are able to hear it. God gave Noah explicit instructions concerning the ark and His intentions for the earth. Being the only one preparing for a storm that no one else could see coming could not have been easy. Noah must have taken tremendous abuse and endured terrible conflict to follow the instructions he was given. But in the end, because of Noah's obedience, him and his family were saved. Sometimes following God's instructions, is not just for your own wellbeing, but also your loved ones.

Right now, you are laying down a new foundation, one that will sustain you through tough times. A foundation built on the love of Jesus and wanting to do as He instructs.

"Jesus replied, 'Anyone who loves Me will obey My teaching.'
-John 14:23

In what areas are you not being obedient? What is causing you to resist changing or making it difficult to sustain the change? Ask God to free to you.

Day 14

Walk with God- Getting back on the path after a stumble

"Then I acknowledged my sin to you and did not cover up my iniquity, I said, 'I will confess my transgressions to the Lord'- and you forgave the guilt of my sin."-Psalm 32:5

Even with your best intentions, we are going to sin against God. The important thing is to acknowledge your mistake and ask for forgiveness. The sooner you do this the less hold it will have over you. Sin eats away at you. It brings guilt and shame. The longer you allow it to stay within you the more damage it does. The best solution- take it to God and He will take away all the guilt and shame.

"Repent, then, and turn to God, so that your sins may be wiped out, that times of refreshing may come from the Lord." -Acts 3:19

Repentance is defined as to feel or express sincere regret or remorse about one's wrongdoing or sin. Be sincere in your request for forgiveness, have confidence you are forgiven and be refreshed.

You are two weeks into this process. Reflect on the changes God has made in your life. Trust in the Lord's plan.

"Trust in the Lord with all your heart and lean not to your own understanding; in all your ways acknowledge Him, and He will make your paths straight."
-Proverbs 3:5-6

What are the next steps in the direction God is leading you? Do not try to understand the plan just follow it.

Know Your identity in Christ

"But I will establish my covenant with you, and you will enter the ark"
-Genesis 6:18

Day 15

Who you are in Christ

"Therefore, if anyone is in Christ, he [she] is a new creation; the old has gone, the new has come!" -II Corinthians 5:17

Noah knew who he was in God. It gave him confidence to know when the Lord was speaking to him. He had no doubt or question about the instructions he was given or think he could not do the task. He did not ask if he was good enough or think "Why me?". He simply listened and obeyed.

You are not who you were before. You are changed. "For we are God's workmanship, created in Christ Jesus to do good works, which God prepared in advance for us to do." -Ephesians 2:10

You have a good work to do. God has instruction for you, but you must know who you are Christ to gain confidence that you are up for the task. You are God's creation. Open your heart and mind to accept who you are in Christ. Dismiss the negativity the devil puts in your mind of who you once were. Decide today you are going to see yourself as God sees you.

Over the next week, you are going to reflect on how God sees you. Begin by thinking about things that seems to come easy to you.

"Yet, O Lord, you are our Father. We are the clay; you are the potter; we are all the work of Your hand."
-Isaiah 64:8

What things bring you joy? Look at yourself in a new light. See the gifts and talents God has given you.

Day 16

You are Special

"For you created my inmost being; you knit me together in my mother's womb." -Psalm 139:13

You were not made by accident. Everything about you has been woven together by God in a special way to create the person you are.

"I praise you because I am fearfully and wonderfully made; your works are wonderful, I know that full well." -Psalm 139:14

In Hebrew, fearfully means with great reverence, heartfelt and with respect. Wonderfully means unique and set apart. If this is how God has created you, then this is how you should see yourself. Do not think any less of who you are.

Go back and look at those areas you outlined yesterday that you instinctually gravitate toward. Identifying your gifts is important as you move forward in discovering what God has called you to do.

"Each one should use whatever gift he [she] has received to serve others, faithfully administering God's grace in it various forms."
-I Peter 4:10

Were you able to toss aside the negativity and see your uniqueness? Can you now appreciate your individuality?

Day 17

You are Valuable

"For you are a people holy to the Lord your God. Out of all the peoples on the face of the earth, the Lord has chosen you to be His treasured possession."
-Deuteronomy 14:2

What makes something valuable to you? Is it how much money or time you spent on it? Is it because other people have deemed it worth something? Now how about what makes a person valuable to you? Is it the amount of time you have invested in the relationship? Or is it just because they are your parent, child or other relative? There are many different reasons you have decided something, or someone is valuable. No matter what the reason you protect it, care for it, and keep it safe. God feels the same for you and will do the same for you. It is not because of anything you've done or because you deserve it. He simply cares about you and values your existence. Because of that, He does not want you to concern yourself with anything. God will provide for all of your needs, because He cares about everything that you care about even the small things.

I'm sure you love the big gestures of appreciation you get from a loved one, but what about the little things people do for you just because they care. Sometimes those things feel even better. Think about something small that you really wanted but thought it was so insignificant you didn't even ask God for it. Maybe you really wanted a nice day for a family outing and the weather report called for rain. But when the day arrived there was nothing but clear skies. Yes, God can do that for you.

"Look at the birds of the air, they do not sow or reap or store away in barns, and yet your heavenly Father feeds them. Are you not much more valuable than they?"
-Matthew 6:26

Reflect on all the small things God has done to show you He cares.

Day 18

You are Important

"Now you are the body of Christ and each of you is a part of it." -I Corinthians 12:27

In I Corinthians 12:12-31, Paul describes the importance of each member of the body of Christ. Just as our physical bodies have many parts with each having its own duty and purpose so does the body of Christ. No part is greater than the other, each is important and needed. Do not feel lesser of yourself because you think your gift is not as glamorous or exciting as someone else's. Do not compare yourself to anyone else. There is only one you for a reason. There is something inside you that only you have, and God wants to use it. Have confidence and joy in knowing that no matter your part to play- you are important and without you the job will not get done the way God designed it.

Read I Corinthians 12:12-31. Let God reveal to you your part in the body. Give thanks for your gifts and the role you have in furthering His kingdom.

"If one part suffers, every part suffers with it; if one part is honored, every part rejoices with it."
-I Corinthians 12:26

Go forward today with a new outlook. Discover ways to use your gifts more in your everyday life.

Day 19

You have Purpose

"And we know that in all things God works for the good of those who love Him, who have been called according to His purpose." -Romans 8:28

It is hard to know what your purpose is. There are so many areas of need it is mind-blowing. You can be so excited about a task and think it is the right thing for you, to later have it fizzle out and not understand why. When you receive God's purpose for your life, let it drive you. Everyday trials will weigh you down but keep your eager willingness to complete God's purpose in your life. Pray daily for renewed strength.

"Now finish the work, so that your eager willingness to do it may be matched by your completion of it, according to your means." -II Corinthians 8:11

The road is not going to be smooth, but you will not be alone. God will be right by your side giving you everything you need. "For if the willingness is there, the gift is acceptable according to what one has, not according to what he does not have." -II Corinthians 8:12

"I believe you have made known to me the path of life; I will find joy in Your presence, with eternal pleasures at your right hand."
-Psalm 16:11

How does God want to use you for His purpose? You may not have the answer just yet- but start asking and meditating on God's word so He will reveal it to you.

Day 20

You are Competent

"Such confidence as this is ours through Christ before God. Not that we are competent in ourselves to claim anything for ourselves, but our competence comes from God" -II Corinthians 3:4-5

When God reveals His purpose to you, it may be a bit overwhelming. You may be tempted to believe that it is impossible. Do not allow that thinking to take over. Do not get caught up in your circumstances and allow it to dictate what you are capable of. God's ability to use you is not based on your education, status, finances, or any other box society places you in. The Lord sees the real you and knows what you can do if you allow Him to lead you. God has given you everything you need to get the job done. Rely on Him for success. A great example is Moses, he was not a great speaker or out going in any way, but God wanted to use Moses to free his people from slavery. Moses had to trust God to make him strong in his weakness. He had to step out in faith that God would do what He said He would do and know that the Lord was by his side. God will do the same for you. When we are weak, He is strong.

Take time to read Exodus chapter 3 and see how God chose Moses even when Moses felt he did not have the necessary skills or abilities to do what God was asking of Him.

"And God said, 'I will be with you. And this will be the sign to you that it is I who have sent you: When you have brought the people out of Egypt, you will worship God on this mountain."
-Exodus 3:12

Is there something God wants you to do, but you have been questioning if you can do it? Write down the reasons why you think you are not qualified or don't have the right skills. And then give them over to God.

Day 21

You are Loved

"For God so loved the world that He gave His one and only Son, that whoever believes in Him shall not perish but have eternal life." -John 3:16

You hear this verse used and even see it on posters in sports stadiums. But you must not be desensitized to it. It is so powerful. The love that God has for you is nothing short of amazing. If you have a child or even if you do not, imagine for a second, sacrificing your child. Someone you love so dearly you would give your own life for. Then add to that, doing it for people that do not even know you, for that matter for those that hate you. It is unfathomable to do such a thing. But that is exactly what God did for you. If you find yourself questioning your self-worth, think about that. You are loved, valued, important, special, competent, and have great purpose. Do not let the devil convince you that you are not. "The thief [devil] comes only to steal and kill and destroy; I have come that they may have life and have it to the full. -John 10:10

God is love. Everything He does is with love intended to do what is best for you. He loves you enough to tell you "No" to things that you think you need or want, but God knows are not best. Trust in His will and follow His example of love. Once you feel God's love, you will want to share it with those around you.

"We love because He first loved us."
-I John 4:19

Take time to truly reflect on what God did for you by sending Jesus to the cross. The sacrifice He made to save you. The pain God put Jesus through so you could have eternal life. And the willingness of Jesus to endure it.

Your Storm has Purpose

"I will send rain on the earth for forty days and forty nights"
-Genesis 7:4

Day 22

You Will Persevere

"You did not choose me, but I chose you and appointed you to go and bear fruit- fruit that will last. Then the Father will give you whatever you ask in My name." -John 15:16

Over the past 21 days, you have worked to strengthen your relationship with God, build trust in Him and gain confidence in yourself and your ability to hear His voice.

As you are working on changing your habits and perceptions that are detrimental to your walk with God, you have most likely encountered many obstacles that have hindered your progress or outright set you back. That is okay. God understands and forgives.

This is a time of preparation. God is preparing you for great things. Allow Him to continue to work in you to create "good soil". (Luke 8:15) Do not let situations around you deter you from your commitment.

Now is the time to stay strong in the things that need to be done. Do not waiver when things get tough, or you are filled with self-doubt. Be confident in your decisions.

"You need to persevere so that when you have done the will of God, you will receive what He has promised."
-Hebrews 10:36

Remind yourself today of what you have committed to do and encourage yourself that God is with you helping you every step of the way.

Day 23

You have a Calling

"I pray also that the eyes of your heart may be enlightened in order that you may know the hope to which He has called you, the riches of His glorious inheritance in the saints." -Ephesians 1:18

God has placed a call on your life. The objective is to get to a place where we are ready to hear it. At this point, you have established or re-established your relationship with God and your commitment to Him. God HAS spoken to you. Perhaps He has called you before in your life and you weren't ready to accept it. You know when the call comes. It tugs at your heart. It stays with you even when you try to ignore it. God will bring it back to you through whatever means He needs to. Your calling does not go away just because you have chosen to ignore it. "For God's gifts and His call are irrevocable." -Romans 11:29

You may be doubtful that you able to do what God has called you to do. But remember, God is strong where you are weak, and you can do all things through Christ who strengthens you. (Philippians 4:13) He would not ask you to do anything you are not capable of.

Everyone's abilities are not the same. You are given what you can handle and as you accomplish each step you will be given more. Do not continue to stay in the same place. Put to work the gifts God has given you. Read Matthew 25:14-29.

"Well done, good and faithful servant! You have been faithful with a few things; I will put you in charge of many things."
-Matthew 25:21

Examine what you are doing with what you have been given. What can you do to be ready to handle more?

Day 24

Have an expectant heart

"And without faith it is impossible to please God, because anyone who comes to Him must believe that He exists and that He rewards those who earnestly seek Him." -Hebrews 11:6

Through faith, open your heart to hear from God and expect that He will answer. Have confidence. Tell yourself, "I will hear God's voice!"

It has taken years of disappointments and loss to bring you to you where you are today. You are done going through life with no direction. You are ready to reconstruct your identity starting with building a new foundation. That takes faith. Faith that God has something better for you because let me tell you, He does.

Through faith those feelings of insecurity and fear will lessen, and you persevere despite them so you can receive what God has promised you. (Hebrews 10:36)

Don't let your sins get in your way. Forgive yourself for the mistakes and hurt you've caused, accept God's forgiveness. And expect to hear God's voice. A clean heart is an open heart.

Read Hebrews 11. Reflect on the examples of great faith.

"Now faith is being sure of what we hope for and certain of what we do not see."
-Hebrews 11:1

Find your motivation to exercise your faith. What will you do today to step out in faith?

Day 25

Be Prepared

"And who knows but that you have come to your royal position for such a time as this?" -Esther 4:14

God is in control. He placed Esther as queen to save her people, but she had to be up for the task. The same is true for you. God will place you where you need to be at the right time. He is preparing you for a great work. Will you be ready? "Do your best to present yourself to God as one approved, a workman who does not need to be ashamed and who correctly handles the word of truth." -II Timothy 2:15

Be ready for God's work through studying His word, prayer, praise, and worship. In these activities, God will reveal His plan for you.

By preparing your heart and mind, you will be ready for the task and have confidence it is from God.

Read I John 4:1-6. Pray to recognize the Spirit of God. Continue exploring the truths in God's word.

"Dear friends, do not believe every spirit, but test the spirits to see whether they are from God, because many false prophets have one out into the world."
-I John 4:1

Write down a meaningful scripture(s) for you to refer to in times of struggle.

Day 26

Know the Truth

"Then you will know the truth, and the truth will set you free." -John 8:32

The truth is God loves you unconditionally, you are on the right path and God's will shall be done in your life if you allow it. "Father if you are willing, take this cup from me; yet not my will, but Yours be done." -Luke 22:42

Jesus was in great agony over dyeing on the cross, but He was still willing to do it because it was what His father put Him on earth to do. There will be things God asks you to do that will be difficult, but you must persevere and see it through for God's glory.

For God's will to be done in your life, you must pray over whatever plans you may have had for yourself and ask if that is His plan. Receive the truth of what your life is meant to be. Wipe away the picture you have for yourself and let God create the picture for your life.

"But when he, the Spirit of truth, comes he will guide you into all truth. He will not speak on his own; he will speak only what he hears, and he will tell you what is yet to come."
-John 16:13

Reflect on John 16:13. Allow the Spirit of truth to fill you. What truths have been revealed?

Day 27

Move from Wanting to Being

"Ask and it will be given to you; seek and you will find; knock and the door will be opened to you. For everyone who asks receives; he who seeks finds; and to him who knocks, the door will be opened." -Luke 11:9-10

Being the person, you are striving to be takes action. All it takes to transform yourself from wanting to be who God has called you to be and being who He has called you to be is action. It is okay to ask for what you want but keep your prayers in line with God's word.

Adopt your new thinking to your everyday life. Every day you have the opportunity to be the person you want to be one step at time, one choice at a time. It will be a conscious effort in the beginning, but with each better decision you make, the effort lessens until it is natural. There will be many forks in the road. Be confident that you will reach your destination through consistent prayer and daily devotion.

"Being confident in this, that He who began a good work in you will carry it on to completion until the day of Christ Jesus.
-Philippians 1:6

What areas do you want to make different choices and what will those new choices be? What actions will you take to "start being"?

Day 28

God Will Give You Rest

"Come to me, all you who are weary and burdened, and I will give you rest."
-Matthew 11:28

The things that have weighed you down are not going to instantaneously disappear. It will take effort on your part to put them down and give them over to God. You will struggle with past thoughts and actions. You will need to reassure yourself daily that this is attainable and will be worth the effort. The burdens you are carrying are heavy, but God wants to take them from you. (Matthew 11:29-30)

Seek God's presence to find peace. Create an environment that allows that. Let it be free from distractions and interruptions. Praise and worship music is a good place to start. Allow the words to fill your heart and put you in the right attitude to be healed. (Psalm 100) For some the exertion of running, walking, or exercising releases endorphins that create feelings of thanksgiving and gratefulness. And at your very lowest, all you need to do is cry out and God will hear you. (Psalm 18:6)

""The Lord replied, 'My Presence will go with you, and I will give you rest.'"
-Exodus 33:14

In His presence is fullness of joy. (Psalm 16:11) Experiment with what works for you to get into His presence regularly to regain peace and find rest. Where will you start?

Be who God wants You to Be

"And Noah did all that the Lord commanded him."
-Genesis 7:5

Day 29

Good Soil

"But the seed on good soil stands for those with a noble and good heart, who hear the word, retain it, and by persevering produce a crop." -Luke 8:15

Through this journey, you have given your life and plans over to God. You have discovered your true identity in Christ. You have made a habit of taking time to cultivate a relationship with God. You are seeing a difference in your attitude and choices. You are making your life a representation of good soil.

At this point, you have examined your life in order to get rid of unwanted behaviors, things that have been holding you back from hearing God's voice. So, now let's look at taking on new behaviors? The fruit of Spirit is an excellent place to start.

Over the next several days, you are going to examine each fruit and reflect on how it is or isn't present in your life. To begin, thoroughly read Galatians 5:22-23. Look at each fruit and take an inventory of your heart.

"You did not choose me, but I chose you and appointed you to go and bear fruit- fruit that last. Then the Father will give you whatever you ask in My name."
-John 15:16

What areas do you feel come through in you and what areas perhaps not so much? Then be open to tackle the areas that need a little work.

Day 30

Love

"Love is patient, love is kind. It does not envy, it does not boast, it is not proud. It is not rude, it is not self-seeking, it is not easily angered, it keeps no record of wrongs. Love does not delight in evil by rejoices with the truth. It always protects, always trusts always hopes, always perseveres."

-I Corinthians 13:4-7

Reflect on the opening verses. Think about what true love is and what it is not. To exhibit love for others in your life, you must first have God's love in your heart. "But God demonstrates His own love for us in this: While we were still sinners, Christ died for us." -Romans 5:8 There is no greater love. Take time to receive and experience the love God has for you.

Love is a decision that you choose to express through your actions. It is a commitment. It is not based on feelings or emotions. You do what is best for those around you not because you feel like it, but because God instructs you to. (I John 4:7-8) Sometimes that means making tough decisions. It means sacrifice.

"And He has given us this command: Whoever loves God must also love his broter."
-I John 4:21

Read I John 4:7-21. Reflect on God's love for you and how you can better express that love to others. Pray for God to cleanse your heart of selfish motivations.

Day 31

Joy

"Do not grieve, for the joy of the Lord is your strength." -Nehemiah 8:10

Having joy is not the absence of hurt. Joy is not allowing grief to consume your spirit. Pure joy is not based on circumstance or event. It is constant. Having joy in your heart brings comfort even in awful times.

One way to keep your joy is by allowing God to help you through your journaling. Journaling is a safe way to deal with the hurt you are experiencing. There are many different things that can cause you grief, but writing down your feelings of hurt, betrayal and sadness will help you work through them and bring areas to light that you perhaps did not even know existing. Everyone deals with pain in their own way, but the result must be healing. Crying is very effective. Not just a few tears, the crying that drains and cleanses your soul and allows God to heal you.

We have all experienced loss in our life from the loss of a loved one, a relationship, a job to losing everything. No matter how bad your situation seems to you God is there waiting for you to call on Him to restore your joy and move you forward.

"Consider it pure joy, my brothers, whenever you face trials of many kinds, because you know that the testing of your faith develops perseverance."
-James 1:2

What is weighing on your heart? Release it today. Write it down and give it over to God. Let Him restore your joy.

Day 32

Peace

"Do not be anxious about anything, but in everything, by prayer and petition, with thanksgiving, present your requests to God. And the peace of God, which transcends all understanding." -Philippians 4:6-7

There are several things that can steal your peace: worry, fear, lack of knowledge, uncertainty, pain and even unforgiveness. The best way to tackle these situations is with scripture. When worry and doubt creep in, when you're afraid to move forward, when you do not understand, or when it is just too painful that is when the only thing you can do is rely on God's word. Speak to the devil just as Jesus did when He was tempted in the desert. You cannot allow Satan to come in and take what is rightfully yours.

"Cast your cares on the Lord and He will sustain you; He will never let the righteous be shaken." -Psalm 55:22

"When I am afraid, I put my trust in You." -Psalm 56:3

Read Psalm 23 and use it when you are feeling overwhelmed. Meditate on it and allow the words to get into your spirit.

"Peace I leave with you; My peace I give you. I do not give to you as the world gives. Do not let your hearts be troubled and do not be afraid."
-John 14:27

Express what is troubling you. Pray over it and feel God's peace in your situation. He is always there for you.

Day 33

Patience

"Wait for the Lord; be strong and take heart and wait for the Lord."
-Psalm 27:14

Patience is determined in HOW we wait. Are you unsatisfied until you get what you want? Do you grumble and moan because your prayers are not answered right away? If it takes too long, do you try to figure it out your own way? Think about these questions and reflect on how you wait when you pray for something. Learn to be content. (Philippians 4:12)

When you ask for something, be fully capable of waiting for God's timing to provide. There is a time for everything, and He will make everything beautiful in its time. (Ecclesiastes 3:1; 3:11) All you have to do is trust in His process. And that will create patience.

Another way to encourage patience in your life is thankfulness. Develop an attitude of gratitude. See all the beauty around you. Shift your focus. Take time to enjoy where God has placed you and learn what He wants you to learn.

"But those who hope [wait] in the Lord will renew their strength. They will soar on wings like eagles; they will run and not grow weary, they will walk and not be faint."
-Isaiah 40:31

What are you thankful for? In your situation, what could God be trying to show you? What lesson(s) may He be trying to teach you? Pray on these questions, let God reveal to you His purpose in your situation.

Day 34

Kindness

"An anxious heart weighs a man down., but a kind word cheers him up."
-Proverbs 12:25

A little kindness goes a long way. You never know how a simple gesture of kindness can affect another person. A smile, a hug, a kind word are ways you can help someone else. Be encouraging even if you don't feel like it. It will come back to you. When the time comes when you need encouragement. God will send someone to you.

Being in a hurry often keeps you from being kind in your daily life. You are rushing out the door to get where you need to be, so you do not have time to engage with other people. You are in a hurry at the grocery store, so you are agitated and sometimes rude. Slowing down and giving yourself enough time opens the door for you to be kind to someone else. Let someone ahead of you line, bringing coffee to a friend, making eye contact with others with a smile are simple gestures that can make a world of difference.

Read Luke 6:27-36 which teaches about how to treat others including your enemies.

"Do to others as you would have them do to you."
-Luke 6:31

What did you take away from these scriptures? What can you do in your daily routine to add more kindness? What can you change to give yourself more time and slow down?

Day 35

Goodness

"Neither do people light a lamp and put it under a bowl. Instead, they put it on its stand, and it gives light to everyone in the house. In the same way, let your light shine before men, that they may see you good deeds and praise your Father in heaven." -Matthew 5:15-16

The Lord wants you to be good, in other words, be holy and pure of heart. Let your light shine. When you are good and doing what is right, naturally you will be helping other people. One of the best ways to improve our situation, is to do good for others. God has placed gifts inside you to use to help others in ways only you can. Get out there and do good.

"Each one should use whatever gifts he has received to serve others, faithfully administering God's grace in its various forms." -I Peter 4:10

Read the parable Jesus told of the good Samaritan in Luke 10:25-37. Reflect on the lesson it teaches about being willing to help others God puts in our path.

"Therefore, as we have the opportunity, let us do good to all people, especially to those who belong to the family to of believers."
-Galatians 6:10

What opportunities does God present for you to help? Look for those today.

Day 36

Gentleness

"Let your gentleness be evident to all. The Lord is near." -Philippians 4:5

Remembering what you read yesterday, the good Samaritan is an excellent example of gentleness as well. He saw a man badly beaten on the side road and chose to stop and help. It did not matter who the man was or where he came from. He was in need, so the Samaritan helped him.

"He went to him and bandaged his wounds, pouring on oil and wine. Then he put him on his own donkey, took him to an inn and took care of him." -Luke 10:34

The Samaritan "took care of him". He would have had to be gentle and caring to tend to such massive wounds. His heart was open to help a complete stranger.

Is heart open to see the needs around you?

"Therefore, as God's chosen people, holy and dearly loved, clothe yourselves with compassion, kindness, humility, gentleness and patience."
-Colossians 3:12

Reflect on any opportunities God put in your path yesterday to help someone. Did you help? Let your heart be open again to help someone today.

Day 37

Faithfulness

"Perseverance must finish its work so that you may be mature and complete, not lacking anything." -James 1:4

Faithfulness requires perseverance and follow through even in the most difficult times. I am sure you are working toward a goal that is what makes life meaningful and interesting. Whether its financial, emotional, physical there are goals to be made. The road to getting there takes commitment. That commitment happens every day. Remind yourself of the prize. Visualize the achievement. Have confidence that through Christ you will achieve your goal.

The toughest time to show faithfulness is in your trials when the road gets tough. You WILL be tempted and feel like giving up or giving in that is when you must lean on God to help you through because He is faithful and will always be there. In addition, He will always provide you a way out. (I Corinthians 10:13)

How awesome is that? So, when temptation comes, do not focus on your weakness focus on God and let Him show you your way out. Your time of suffering is a chance to deepen your relationship with Christ. Do not be discouraged by the daunting mountain you face, instead allow the Lord to be by your side to take one more step and face one more day until you get there. Don't let this hard time be in vain. Use it for God's glory.

"You need to persevere so that when you have done the will of God, you will receive what He has promised."
-Hebrews 10:36

Review the goals you have set for what you wanted to accomplish from this journey. Be encouraged by your progress.

Day 38

Self-Control

"A fool gives full vent to his anger, but a wise man keeps himself under control." -Proverbs 29:11

Having self-control is extremely important. Your feelings can create emotions that lead to wrong actions. Be mindful of what you are trying to achieve within yourself. Instead, let wisdom control your actions. Let a pure heart motivate your behavior.

"For this reason, make every effort to add to your faith goodness; and to goodness knowledge; and to knowledge, self-control; and to self-control, perseverance; and to perseverance, godliness; and to godliness, brotherly kindness; and to brotherly kindness, love." -II Peter 1:5-7

Consistency in your actions builds character and integrity. Part of living in faithfulness comes from self-control. Choose to exercise restraint and not succumb to temptation. You will be an example of God's work in your life. (A work in progress, but a good work) God understands you will mess up. You will cave-in to temptation or lose your cool. But the wonderful thing about God is that He is always there to forgive you and help you overcome your challenges. All you have to do is ask.

"But I discipline my body and keep it under control, lest after preaching to others I myself should be disqualified."
-I Corinthians 9:27(ESV)

When do you find your behavior hard to control? What can you do differently in those situations? Are there areas you are tempted more often? Ask God to help you exert discipline.

Day 39

Go and bear fruit

"I am the vine; you are the branches. If a man remains in Me and I in him, he will bear much fruit; apart from Me you can do nothing." -John 15:5

As God flooded the earth for forty days, the ark rose higher and higher above the earth. The ark floated on the surface of the water. (Genesis 7:18) Noah and his family had to deal with the constant rocking and the ups and downs of the rising water. The same holds true in your life. You will be dealing with life's ups and downs as you navigate through your new identity. Remain in Jesus and allow Him to help you carry out the characteristics He wants you to display- the fruits of the Spirit. You have worked hard to get here. You dedicated yourself daily to meditating on God's word and hearing His calling for your life. You are ready to live a new life.

Meditate on John 15:1-17. Allow God to strengthen you and embrace the confidence He gives to "bear much fruit". Go out and show the difference God has made in your life and let others know He can do the same for them.

"This is My command: Love each other."
-John 15:17

What takeaways did you gather from the passage? As you near the end of this journey, reflect on your new direction and how far you have come.

Day 40

Embracing your new identity and living on purpose

"No good tree bears bad fruit, nor does a bad tree bear good fruit. Each tree is recognized by its own fruit." -Luke 6:43-44

You have spent forty days reconstructing your identity. The rain has stopped, but this is not the end. It was almost a year after the flood waters stopped before the dove came back with an olive leaf. Live out God's plan daily. Take what God has called you to do and live on purpose. Use everything you have worked on and continue one day at a time.

The Lord is moving in your life and the devil is trying to deter you. Stand firm on God's word. Remind the devil who you are in Christ, and that He has a plan for you.

"Then Noah built an alter to the Lord and, taking some of the clean animals and clean birds, he sacrificed burnt offerings on it. The Lord smelled the pleasing aroma and said in His heart: "Never again will I curse the ground because of man, even though every inclination of his heart is evil from childhood. And never again will I destroy all living creatures, as I have done." -Genesis 8:20-21

Your offering is between you and God. Allow Him to show you what He wants and reveal to you His promise. Go forward and live on purpose!!

"Whenever the rainbow appears in the clouds, I will see it and remember the everlasting covenant between God and all living creatures of every kind on the earth."
-Genesis 9:16

Finishing thoughts

God has a purpose and plan for your life. He wants your life to be complete and fulfilled. I am sure through this journey; God has revealed so many amazing things to you. Use your journal to refer back to those revelations when you need encouragement. This is the beginning of a deeper, more mature relationship with God. God is pleased with your faith to begin this journey and your perseverance to finish. Take the concepts you have learned and develop them. Make them part of your everyday life.

> *"By faith Noah, when warned about things not yet seen, in holy fear built an ark to save his family. By his faith he condemned the world and became heir of the righteousness that comes by faith." -Hebrews 11:7*

Made in the USA
Middletown, DE
30 April 2023